John Bradbury lives in Australia, where he teaches and coaches the concepts described in this book. After working in both the UK and Australia in various leadership positions over a twenty-year period, John realised that the culture in a workplace is something that takes a lot of effort to get right. He started his own business, Workplace Culture, to address this significant challenge that leaders face. The tools of his trade are coaching accreditation with Integral Coaching Canada and a licence to practise the Collaborative Way® team-development program. If you would like to further develop and explore the practices in this book, John can be contacted via his website, www.workplaceculture.com.au. You can also become part of a collaborative community by joining the "I Collaborate" group on Facebook.

I
COLLABORATE

Strategies and coaching practices
for leaders

John Bradbury

First published in Australia in 2018
by Workplace Culture Pty Limited
ABN 87 152 494 865
workplaceculture.com.au

ISBN 9780 6483 3689 1 (paperback)
ISBN 9780 6483 3688 4 (ebook)

Editing and design by Solas Text & Design
Cover image © shutterstock.com

* * *

For Lindsay and Lily

* * *

Contents

Preface

This book is for anyone interested in developing themselves. The behaviours and skills I discuss here all make common sense. However, they are not yet common practice.

I wrote this book because I am inspired to share what I've learned about human relationships and how we can all do better.

I wrote this book because of my belief in the power of collaboration and in our ability to change.

John Bradbury
Coach, teacher, facilitator

Introduction

This book is all about you. It's about your development as a person. It's about taking responsibility for what you create each minute of the day. Learning to improve your interpersonal skills will potentially benefit all your relationships, and many of the strategies and practices in this book relate to communication skills that can be used in a wide range of situations.

However, the material will be particularly beneficial for anyone in a leadership role who wants to improve their interpersonal skills. If you want to become a transformational leader, the journey starts with you. How can you transform yourself to more effectively lead others?

As a leader at any level in an organisation, you are influencing its culture, minute by minute. Every word you utter and every gesture you make potentially has an impact on others. Creating a culture of collaboration in an organisation starts with the individual. The best way to influence the culture is to *be* the culture you would like to experience. This is a powerful way to take responsibility.

Adopting this approach brings a focus to the workplace on who you are as a person, as well as on what you do. When members of a group observe these two facets of their leader, existing side by side, the chances of building a successful, high-performing team significantly increase. So, ask yourself, "How can I develop to positively impact my business and personal relationships?"

Creating a collaborative culture

My aim is to become your collaboration coach, by offering a mixture of challenge and support. The support comes in the form of information about how to be skillfully collaborative. The challenge comes in the form of "coaching practices" that ask you to become more aware of your behaviours and choose to make changes.

I spent over twenty years working in corporate environments, and the one thing that consistently stood out for me was the way that people often went out of their way to undermine each other. I can't claim innocence myself, but I do know that undermining others never leads to a collaborative, successful culture in the workplace. It always has a ripple effect through a team and builds mistrust.

For the last fifteen years I have been working as an independent coach, helping organisations build a more collaborative culture in their workplaces. I find this very rewarding work and I wrote this book to share some of my experience in coaching and teaching collaboration skills.

After gaining accreditation with Integral Coaching Canada and becoming a licensed facilitator of the Collaborative Way® team-development program, I have been applying my skills in organisations as a change agent in service of business outcomes. The approach I take embraces both individual and team development—I have found that a commitment to both is required to effect any significant change.

This book contains elements of The Collaborative Way®, and I have blended this information with my coaching experience to create a number of "coaching practices" to support leaders in their growth and development.

If you are serious about leading change, taking the approach "I'm just fine as I am, thank you, but you all need to change" is not an effective strategy for getting results. Instead, demonstrating a preparedness to look at yourself, and make changes to the way you work, naturally recruits others into the same mindset.

Building a collaborative team and culture starts from within. It requires a sustained commitment from *you*. This book will show you what it takes and how to make the change in yourself.

If you commit to engaging with the coaching practices in this book, you will develop your skills of collaboration and that will affect those around you, sometimes in a profound way. You might not see the difference in yourself, but others almost certainly will.

Embrace discomfort

When I do coaching work with my clients, one of the requests that I make is that they give themselves permission to be uncomfortable. I know from many years of self-development work that it is natural for us to avoid discomfort and that, paradoxically, when we strive to stay comfortable, we limit our own development.

I remember attending a presentation skills course over two days and I found it to be incredibly uncomfortable. We were repeatedly put in the position of having to present to the group. By the end of the course I realised that I had lost my fear of presenting. I had a new-found confidence and was able to stand up in front of people and talk. Prior to the course, this had been a terrifying thought. Afterwards, the thought of presenting became quite exciting. This wouldn't have happened without embracing my discomfort.

When you engage with the coaching practices in this book, the ones that make you feel uncomfortable are the ones to focus on. Discomfort is an indicator that this is an area worth working on until it no longer creates this feeling in you.

Expect resistance to change

I learn from every coaching client I work with, especially those I find challenging. I recall one client who consistently refused to apply any of the coaching practices we agreed on. I could see that his leadership skills were lacking, and as a way of highlighting this I organised a 360 review—which involves interviewing the person's manager, peers and those who report to them—to give him some constructive feedback.

I then had a conversation with him and pointed out how powerful his resistance to change was. But even after this feedback process, he steadfastly refused to make any changes to his leadership style and, unfortunately, he subsequently lost his job.

This is an extreme example, but I tell this story to highlight that resistance is normal and to be expected.

If you engage with a coaching practice in this book and find yourself going back to your old ways, congratulate yourself on recognising your own resistance to change, and continue your efforts. Resistance is part of the change process.

You may also notice others resisting any change in you that is occurring. It's almost as though they subconsciously prefer what they know—the old you—and when you change and become more collaborative, the new you may not always be welcomed at first.

However, persistence with a collaborative approach will pay dividends in the long run, and you may find that those who don't like to collaborate self-select themselves out of the environment as it changes. I remember one company where I introduced a collaborative approach and several of the team leaders resigned because they didn't want to adopt that approach. They preferred a more autocratic style of leadership and couldn't let that go. Resistance to change, once again.

There's no blame here, though. A collaborative environment isn't for everyone.

The egotistical leader

As a way of highlighting the kind of leader I want to help develop in this book, let's characterise its opposite: the egotistical leader.

The egotistical leader isn't necessarily interested in defining what the team is doing. They are usually more interested in looking good or impressing someone. The bigger picture of delivering on a specific plan and helping others achieve their goals can be a secondary consideration.

Meetings with this leader don't always have a clear purpose; indeed, a productive team meeting is rarely a priority for this kind of leader.

The egotistical leader doesn't have good listening skills or any intention to be a good listener. They are too busy thinking about what they are about to say to spend time listening to you. They are more interested in being heard than doing any listening, and they expect you to understand their intentions and sometimes even read their minds and know what they want.

The egotistical leader has their own version of "speaking straight" (see Chapter 3). This might mean expressing themselves strongly, without any regard for the impact of their speaking; it may even involve "giving someone a piece of their mind" from time to time. The focus is on being heard, not on shared understanding. And if they aren't being heard, the volume gets turned up!

Nor is being for others—expressing your empathy and support for other members of your team (see Chapter 4)—a priority. For the egotistical leader the focus is more on "What's in it for me? How can I get the most out of each situation? How can I look good? How can I score points against my competitors?"

The egotistical leader won't be against indulging in gossip—that is a way for them to make sense of their surroundings—and they aren't concerned with how that gossiping looks from a team member's perspective.

An egotistical leader will expect you to honour your commitments (see Chapter 5). That may include commitments you don't even realise you have made, but which have just been assumed by the egotistical leader. This apparent lack of alignment isn't the leader's fault, of course: you should have realised what the leader wanted and made sure it happened.

The egotistical leader doesn't believe in acknowledgment and appreciation (see Chapter 6). That would be a sign of weakness and might send the wrong message, such as, it's okay to relax now and stop trying.

The egotistical leader doesn't worry about inclusion and alignment (see Chapters 7 and 8). They aren't concerned about who is included in a conversation because it's all about them, not about the team. Similarly, alignment isn't necessary, except for alignment with the leader. The expectation is that you simply do what the leader wants.

Blaming is a way of life for this type of leader. As a result, team members tend to focus on how to avoid blame rather than how to achieve positive business outcomes. With no support for collaboration, progress inevitably slows and, in turn, the frustration of the leader increases. Work is no longer enjoyable.

This characterisation is somewhat over the top; however, I'm sure you have all met leaders who had some, though hopefully not all, of these characteristics. It's not necessarily their fault. Most of the time, people in leadership positions are doing the best they can with the skills they have.

One of the reasons for writing this book was to help leaders develop a more collaborative style that will go some way to repairing any damage inflicted by an egotistical approach.

HOW TO USE THIS BOOK

The book is comprised of a series of chapters, each of which introduces a different aspect of working collaboratively. Work through it as follows:

1. Read the book from start to finish, making note of the pages where you find collaboration strategies and coaching practices that you would like to work on.

2. Choose one or two coaching practices to focus on. These should be those that will challenge you and create some discomfort for you.

3. Use a journal to write notes as you engage with the practices in the book. Journalling facilitates the process of looking at yourself and making choices in your behaviour. What is internal is effectively made external on a piece of paper and is more easily reviewed.

4. Answer the coaching questions for each coaching practice in your journal. These questions are there to help you understand your own internal processing and to see the shifts that are occurring within you.

5. Refer to the journal each day to remind yourself which skill you are currently focusing on developing.

6. Continually looking for opportunities to apply the coaching practices will accelerate your learning and development. Engage with each practice until you believe you have learned the new behaviour.

CHAPTER 1

Defining Your Goals

Reviewing what your team does and doesn't do well. Involving team members in this process. Examining the way you work together and discussing how you should move ahead. Creating a shared vision.

Do you routinely define team and individual goals and desired outcomes? Are you revisiting these goals regularly and updating them as necessary? Does everyone understand each other's priorities?

* * *

To practise collaboration requires something to collaborate on; however, exactly what that is isn't always well defined.

Let's use meetings as an example: when the focus of a meeting is clear to participants, they are more likely to make a valuable contribution that is relevant to the current challenges. This clarity creates the right environment for great collaboration.

Contrast this with meetings that have poor or no definition of the agenda and goals, where you are likely to hear comments such as, "What was that all about?", "Meetings are a waste of time" and "Why was I invited?"

▶ **COLLABORATION STRATEGY**

Regularly review your aims

Are you and your team clear about what your goals are today, tomorrow, this week, this month and for the next year? It's absolutely crucial this structure is understood and visible so that shared understanding and alignment is present in the team. Such clarity provides direction, motivation, engagement and a feeling of belonging. Without goals and plans, a team will be firefighting and directionless, at best.

COACHING PRACTICE
Creating a review process
Review the plans and goals you and your team have in place. Are these priorities continually reviewed? If you don't have regular reviews, create a schedule to do so. These meetings will be an opportunity to continually reassess the team's direction.

Explain your reasons for doing this. Let the team know their buy-in and alignment is important to you. This, in turn, could raise questions about resources and priorities, so it's a good idea to think about these topics before the first meeting.

QUESTIONS AND OBSERVATIONS
* How do team members react to the subject and to your explanation of why you want a regular meeting?
* Is there any resistance to having such a discussion?
* Do you need to meet any team members one-on-one to address their concerns?

▶ COLLABORATION STRATEGY
Make becoming a more collaborative leader a high priority
The obvious place to start creating a collaborative culture is where you have most influence—on yourself. The first step is to decide that you will take personal responsibility for the culture you create around you. Waiting for others to become collaborative doesn't work.

The choices you make as a leader ripple out through your organisation because you influence others just by being in a leadership position. In fact, the unwritten part of each person's job description is "watch the leader"; so everything you do is scrutinised, whether you like it or not.

COACHING PRACTICE
Examining your collaborative mindset
Start to notice when you are not engaging or collaborating with others. When do you make decisions in isolation? When do you decide on actions without discussing them with others? Choose a decision each

day that you might normally make alone, and consult with one person who will be affected by that decision.

QUESTIONS AND OBSERVATIONS
- How did you react to this practice?
- How did the person you consulted react?
- What benefits can you see in making decisions this way in the future?
- Is there any downside to involving others in the decision-making process?

►COLLABORATION STRATEGY
Make sure meetings have a clear purpose
Most people will have attended very effective meetings, and also meetings that were a waste of time. One of the elements of a successful meeting is that it has a clear purpose.

COACHING PRACTICE
Declaring your objectives
At every meeting you attend, ensure that the purpose of the meeting has been declared at the beginning. If it's your meeting, send out an agenda at least a day before. Better still, ask others to submit agenda items.

If it's not your meeting, ask for an agenda. If an agenda has not been drawn up, ask for the meeting's purpose to be defined at the start of proceedings.

QUESTIONS AND OBSERVATIONS
- What resistance do you notice to this practice?
- Does pushing this requirement create any discomfort in you or others? If so, why is that the case?

►COLLABORATION STRATEGY
Tell stories to bring your vision to life
If you want to enrol others in a project, tell stories that reflect your ideas and goals. People remember stories more easily than data. Don't limit

yourself to discussing what *you* will be doing. Talk about the journey and the reasons why you need others to assist you and what each of them can bring to the team. If a person understands that their skills are required and appreciated, they are much more likely to support a project and get involved.

COACHING PRACTICE
Setting the scene
Think of the team you are leading. Consider its goals and how these can be achieved. Take the time to tell team members what they bring to the group, how they can all assist you and each other, and why you need them. Describe some scenarios where each team member has added value to the team. These examples should demonstrate the sort of behaviours you are looking for and be linked to the achievement of specific goals.

QUESTIONS AND OBSERVATIONS
• What impact do these descriptions have on the team?
• What impact does this have on you?
• If your team members are in leadership positions themselves, can you suggest they use this approach with their own teams?

||||||||||||||||||||||||||||||||||||||||||||||||||||||||||||||||||||||||||||||||||||||||||||||||||||||||||||||||||||||||||||||||||||||||||||||||||||

PERSONAL EXPERIENCE

I have worked as a senior leader within many teams in manufacturing. The times when I was part of a team whose goals were clearly defined and constantly updated were when I felt most motivated and had the greatest job satisfaction. There were many other characteristics that defined this team, but the clarity around goals was one of the major components of success. In contrast, teams that I was part of earlier in my career that had ill-defined goals tended to be more reactive and focused on firefighting.

Some years ago, I was a keen cyclist and would cycle a minimum of 30 kilometres most days. What kept me engaged and motivated was having goals to improve my times over various distances. I found that I was most motivated when I had a goal I had not yet reached but believed I was capable of achieving.

The same applied in my working life. The times when I was given realistic goals, and had some involvement in setting them, were the times when I was most engaged in my work.

‖‖‖

CHAPTER 2

Listening Generously

Learning to listen for the contribution people are making when they speak, rather than listening based on preconceived assessments, opinions and judgments.

Are you consciously using listening as a powerful practice?

* * *

Listening is one of the most underrated practices in leadership. How often do you go about your business with a focus on listening to others? Do you understand and appreciate the power of your listening over the power of your speaking?

People who start to intentionally use listening as a tool soon appreciate its power. Listening builds understanding, engages people, values people, fosters great teamwork, supports others, enables creativity and solves problems.

Learning to be a great listener is a lifelong journey.

When we listen for the contribution in each other's speaking and block out preconceived assessments, opinions and judgments, we use our listening skills in a more powerful way. It doesn't mean we are always going to agree with what is being said; however, this style of listening *will* result in a greater level of understanding of what has been said.

If you want to help those around you, then understanding that the way you listen can have a positive or negative effect is a great place to start.

It is common practice to focus on what you are going to say rather than on bringing a listening presence. I'm sure you've been in a situation where two people are speaking in what appear to be unrelated conversations because neither is listening to the other. In this situation, it only takes one person to start listening to affect both people. As the listener, I now hear what you are saying, and you experience being heard. The whole conversation changes and becomes more productive.

►COLLABORATION STRATEGY
Experiment with listening

Start using your listening as a conscious tool for delivering change. Pay attention to how you listen to people in different contexts. This will give you a greater appreciation of the power and value of listening.

COACHING PRACTICE
Listening to your loved ones

Bring a listening focus to your life away from work. Start with your family and friends. Have a daily practice of just listening to understand, and challenge yourself to listen without comment. No judgments, no criticism. Just listen. Only speak if it is to ask questions to better understand what is being said. This is a great way to hone your listening skills away from work, and those close to you will definitely appreciate it over time.

QUESTIONS AND OBSERVATIONS
- What impact did your listening have at home and with friends?
- Are some people easier to listen to than others?
- Do you find yourself struggling to just listen? If so, why? What is it you want to say?

►COLLABORATION STRATEGY
Use your listening to engage a speaker

Listen for the value in what others are saying. Summarise for the speaker what you think are the important things that they have said. Watch the other person engage as you provide the listening and demonstrate your interest.

COACHING PRACTICE
Listening at work

Spend the day listening as an exercise in discovery. Say as little as possible for a day and encourage others to speak as you listen. Provide feedback on what you've heard. If you are used to speaking a lot, this will be difficult. However, if you make the effort you will undoubtedly learn something about yourself and others. Notice when you stop listening and start speaking.

QUESTIONS AND OBSERVATIONS
- When do you stop listening?
- Do you give up listening to some people but not to others?
- What do you do when you stop listening?
- Can you remember what you were thinking when you stopped listening? By focusing on your internal processes, you can start to improve your listening.

▶COLLABORATION STRATEGY
Check that you have been heard correctly

If you want to be an effective leader, make sure that others understand you. Don't just assume that they do. Action results from what has been heard, not necessarily from what was said. Making sure everyone is on the same page can save a lot of time.

Silence doesn't necessarily convey understanding; in fact, silence is a good indicator of the need to check for understanding. In hierarchical organisations, silence can mean "It's too risky for me to speak up, so I won't say anything." For people in leadership positions, it's important to create an environment that encourages team members to ask questions without feeling embarrassed. When team members are freely asking for clarification, you know that the environment is good. When you check that others have understood what you have said, it demonstrates that you care, not that you think they are being slow to catch on.

COACHING PRACTICE
Building your team's listening skills

Facilitate a short discussion with your team about the process of checking for understanding and how this benefits everyone. Encourage every team member to check for understanding whenever there is any doubt. Explain that people take action based on what they have heard not on what has been said.

• How did team members react to this discussion?
• Can you think of examples where checking for understanding could have saved time in the past?
• Can you think of examples coming up in your diary where it will be important to make sure everyone in the team is on the same page?

▶ COLLABORATION STRATEGY
Meditate to improve your listening
Are you aware of the part of you that is silent, with no chatter? This is who you are when you are being a great listener. It's possible to develop this part of yourself by meditating regularly. If that's something you can make time for, it's very worthwhile.

COACHING PRACTICE
A daily meditation
Commit to a daily ten minutes' meditation initially and increase the duration gradually over a period of months. Try to make it a routine by meditating at the same time daily. The focus of the meditation should be to listen to your surroundings. That's all. Just listen for ten minutes. It's not as easy as it sounds. When you notice yourself drifting, come back to listening. Consider it an achievement just to have sat quietly for the full ten minutes.

QUESTIONS AND OBSERVATIONS
• What do you notice about your listening process?
• What do you observe about your posture during meditation?
• Can you maintain steady, slow breathing as you meditate?

▶ COLLABORATION STRATEGY
Monitor your level of curiosity
When you check your level of curiosity during a conversation, you receive direct feedback on the quality of your listening. You can then use

that feedback to improve your listening. If your curiosity level is low, the chances are that your listening isn't great.

COACHING PRACTICE
Testing your listening skills
Choose someone who you find it hard to listen to and have a conversation with them while trying to keep your level of curiosity high. Ask questions, carefully consider the answers, offer your comments and observations. Notice how easy or difficult it is to maintain curiosity.

QUESTIONS AND OBSERVATIONS
• Did you learn anything about your listening?
• Did you learn anything about the other person?
• What impact did your listening have on you or the speaker?

►COLLABORATION STRATEGY
Admit to not listening
Sometimes we stop listening, but we don't ask someone to repeat what they said or, worse still, we keep nodding as though we have heard and understood. This isn't the way to develop a collaborative culture. Ask the person to repeat what they said and explain that you stopped listening for a second and you want to make sure you have understood. We all stop listening at times. The problem is we think it might be disrespectful to own up to not listening. Noticing when you do and asking someone to repeat what they said is actually respectful.

COACHING PRACTICE
Encouraging honest listening
Discuss the process of listening with your team. Give them permission to ask for things to be repeated. Explain that you understand that everyone stops listening at times; it's just part of being human and not a weakness. You can also explain that you don't want team members to pretend they have heard and understood when they haven't.

- How did the team respond to this discussion?
- How well are your team members listening to each other?
- Can you provide feedback to team members when they don't listen to each other?

▶COLLABORATION STRATEGY
Use listening to resolve conflict
Listening is a fantastic skill for resolving conflict, whether you are a participant in a dispute or facilitating its resolution. What listening does is remove the emotion from the situation. If you choose to be a listener, the other person will feel heard, which will calm them down. When you are listening, it doesn't necessarily mean you are "agreeing"; instead, "understanding" is the goal. And when you have truly understood the other person, you are in a much better place to agree or disagree.

COACHING PRACTICE
Listening as a means of understanding
When you have a disagreement with someone, first drop the need to be right, which is where conflict often begins. If you then shift your attention to listening and maintaining your curiosity, you may start to understand the other person's point of view. Focus on the idea of listening to the facts. This will help you understand both sides of the discussion, and slow the process down. At worst, you might find some areas of agreement; at best, you might find you are arguing over something about which you actually see eye to eye.

QUESTIONS AND OBSERVATIONS
- How did introducing the idea of listening influence the situation?
- Can you clearly explain the other person's point of view?
- Was the conflict resolved? If not, what are the next steps that you need to take (possibly including more listening)?

►COLLABORATION STRATEGY
Listen again

Conflicts frequently arise when two people are arguing about who is right. In most cases both people are partially right, although there can be resistance to seeing this. Learning to switch to listening when you are in the midst of a conflict is challenging.

COACHING PRACTICE
Switching to listening

When you find yourself arguing because you want to be right, stop and switch to listening in order to understand the other person. This will take some practice to do in the moment. The key is to notice when those moments start and catch yourself as you begin your explanation of why you are right and the other person is wrong.

QUESTIONS AND OBSERVATIONS
- How did the other person respond to you?
- Can you see how taking an interest in the perspective of another person can build trust?
- Who are the people with whom you most often have disagreements based on who is right or wrong?

►COLLABORATION STRATEGY
Refrain from interrupting

Have you noticed how annoying it is when someone cuts across you and speaks before you have finished what you are saying? Do you ever do that yourself? How do you respond when someone does that to you? Do you stop listening to them? Do you challenge them to listen?

COACHING PRACTICE
Managing interruptions

Start managing those moments when either you cut across someone else or someone does that to you. In the former case, stop, apologise and say you realise that the other person hadn't finished what they were saying. In the latter, stop the other person and say you hadn't finished what you were saying. In both examples, you are promoting better listening.

QUESTIONS AND OBSERVATIONS
- What happens to you just before you interrupt someone else while they are speaking? What are you saying to yourself? Are you bored? Do you consider you have something more important to say?
- When someone interrupts you, how do you react and what action do you take? Do you consider that behaviour rude or just a symptom of poor listening?

▶ COLLABORATION STRATEGY
Become aware of your filters
Filters are preconceived ideas we have or assumptions we make about how others communicate with us, whether they are individuals or whole departments in an organisation. Here are some examples of filters: "I know what you're going to say", "I have the answer to your problem", "You obviously need my advice", "I've heard this before", "I haven't got time to listen to this." Any filters that are negative in nature get in the way of good listening.

Filters can't be destroyed, they can only be recognised and "suspended" or "parked". (Have you ever tried to stop thinking?)

Once we identify our filters, they have less of a hold over us and we can make more informed choices about people and situations.

COACHING PRACTICE
Parking your filters
Think of a person you find it hard to listen to and make a list of the filters that you have for them. Deliberately have a conversation with that person where you consciously put your filters to one side. Listen as well as you can and ask questions. Be as curious as possible.

QUESTIONS AND OBSERVATIONS
- How did the other person react to your listening without filters?
- Did you hear anything from the person you haven't heard before?

- What sort of impact is your listening having?
- Which other situations would benefit from such high-quality listening?

▶ **COLLABORATION STRATEGY**
Monitor interdepartmental relationships
Does your team experience problems with other departments? If so, it's a clear indication that collaboration is sorely lacking, especially if your team members complain about the other departments or tell unflattering stories about them.

COACHING PRACTICE
Identifying department filters
Have a discussion with your team about how to improve its relationship with another department and explore what the benefits would be. The plan could be simply to make more of an effort in those interdepartmental relationships, or it could involve meeting with the head of the other department to clear the air and create a better atmosphere. The main thing is to take action. The starting point should be to listen to the perspectives of people in the other department, as understanding their perspectives will build bridges and improve the quality of the relationships.

QUESTIONS AND OBSERVATIONS
- What processes could you put in place to ensure the relationships between departments are steadily improved?
- Is there any resistance to improving relationships with another department? Is there any history between the departments that needs to be cleaned up?
- Is there some way that you could facilitate an improvement in the listening that occurs between departments?
- Have you identified any common goals?

▶ **COLLABORATION STRATEGY**
Offer your full attention
If you want to collaborate effectively, you have to be aware of where you

are directing your attention, at all times. If people visit you and find you preoccupied with your computer or phone, they will feel like they are competing for your attention. At best you'll appear inefficient, at worst annoying and disrespectful.

When communicating with anyone, do so with as much attention as possible. If you can do that, and also manage your filters, then you will find yourself very present, in the moment and available for others, and they will definitely notice the difference. I have heard numerous examples of the powerful impact that managing distractions has had on individuals.

COACHING PRACTICE
Managing distractions
Whenever anyone comes to meet with you, ensure that all potential distractions are minimised. Try this with someone you may not have valued highly in the past. Give them your full attention. Shut down or turn away from your computer. Switch your phone off. Make that person the most important subject in your life at that time.

It only takes one person to change a relationship. If you can manage distractions, you will hear more, and the other person will feel heard.

QUESTIONS AND OBSERVATIONS
- What effect is managing distractions having on you and the person you are communicating with?
- What are you actually sacrificing when you manage distractions in this way?
- Can you think of other situations where managing distractions would serve you well?

►COLLABORATION STRATEGY
Notice when you stop listening
Are there any situations where you have given up? Was that with a particular person or with another department, for example? Giving up means you have stopped listening.

COACHING PRACTICE
Not giving up
If there is a situation or a person you have given up on, make a plan to address it. Giving up is a sign that there is an opportunity for collaboration, as well as a reason to reflect on your behaviour. Go back to that situation. Listen again and try to attain understanding.

QUESTIONS AND OBSERVATIONS
- Think back on the situation. What were you not doing or saying and what made you give up?
- How can your use of listening as a tool continue to improve this situation?
- Are there any other situations where you have given up and could take action?

►COLLABORATION STRATEGY
Listen with empathy
As you are listening to someone, think, "What is the value being added right now by this person? What do they care about?"

If you can answer these two questions about the person you are communicating with, then you can connect much more effectively with them and make progress. If you can't answer these questions, there is an opportunity to listen with more curiosity.

COACHING PRACTICE
Gaining another perspective
Choose several conversations in the next week where you will try to bring this level of focus to the discussion and arrive at the point where you can answer the two questions above. To achieve this, you may need to consider other questions, such as "What is this person trying to achieve?", "How can I help them achieve that?", "What's their reason for doing this?"

QUESTIONS AND OBSERVATIONS
- What is the impact of this level of engagement on you and on the other person?

- Do you notice how by listening more carefully you immediately feel more empathy for the other person and gain a clearer understanding of their goals and concerns?
- Who else could you apply this approach to?

||||||||||||||||||||||||||||||||||||||||||||||||||||||||||||||||||||||||||||||||||||||||||||||||||||||||||||||||||||||||||||||||||||||||||||||||

PERSONAL EXPERIENCE

I didn't become fully aware of the power of listening until I started consciously practising listening with a belief that it could truly make a difference. Now I have my own company and I work as a coach and team-development facilitator, I am continually using listening as a tool in my business interactions. I have reached the point where I feel confident that if I simply listen generously, the next steps will become obvious. This practice has resulted in me being open to a wide range of possibilities, rather than believing that I have to have the answers all the time.

That's precisely why listening is a core skill in collaboration and why the topic is dealt with early in this book. Indeed, if I had to choose any skill to work on first to improve someone's leadership, it would be listening.

I remember when I started to pay attention to the impact of my listening (or lack of listening). An early lesson came from my daughter, Lily. She was around six years of age at the time and I would pick her up from school in the afternoon. She was starting to be discerning about what was working in her relationships with the other children at school and what wasn't. She would excitedly relate something that had happened that day and I, being a well-meaning father, would immediately start to give her advice.

On several occasions, this advice was met with an angry response from Lily. It took a few of these reactions to make me realise that all she wanted was for me to listen and understand her. She wasn't looking for advice, she just wanted her story heard and understood.

Lily is now fifteen years old and I still catch myself doing this, but less frequently. I also notice that when I consciously just listen to her, things go much better. I can see the impact of my listening on her, and it's always positive. She clearly feels more valued when I do this.

||||||||||||||||||||||||||||||||||||||||||||||||||||||||||||||||||||||||||||||||||||||||||||||||||||||||||||||||||||||||||||||||||||||||||||||||

CHAPTER 3

Speaking Straight

To speak honestly in a way that makes a positive contribution. Making clear and direct requests. Being willing to propose ideas or take positions that may result in conflict, in order to reach agreed objectives.

Are you paying attention to the impact of your speaking?

* * *

Speaking straight is saying exactly how you see a situation, with the intention of making a positive impact on whatever situation you are in.

In some cases, speaking straight will result in conflict; however, if it is combined with listening generously, it results in a very powerful combination that can help move any situation forwards.

The fear of discomfort and hurting people's feelings is what usually stops someone speaking straight.

▶ COLLABORATION STRATEGY
Take ownership of the impact of your speaking
When you speak straight you are offering your perspective in relation to a particular situation. Your aim should be to make a positive contribution. Sometimes you may notice a negative reaction to what you said, which can be a verbal or non-verbal reaction. This is your cue to explain further what you mean or to ask the person why they have reacted that way.

By doing this, you are again speaking straight because you are taking ownership of the impact of your speaking.

COACHING PRACTICE
Planning your speaking
Apply the following check when you are about to say something: "How

is my speaking going to benefit or support someone?" If the answer
to this question is "It's not", then think about the point you are trying
to make. Can you make this point in a positive way that will benefit
someone or something?

QUESTIONS AND OBSERVATIONS
• What examples can you come up with of your speaking having had a
  negative impact, resulting in some unfinished business?
• Who are the people you find it difficult to speak up with? Why is that?
• Can you read how others react to you?
• Can you see how you could take more ownership of the impact of your
  speaking?

►COLLABORATION STRATEGY
Develop the skill of speaking up
When you care about something, speak up. Speaking up in a way that
makes a positive contribution and at the same time shows a willingness
to challenge others is a skill worth developing.

   It's also worth developing a shared understanding in a team that this
is an effective way to work together. Creating that understanding requires
the leader to role-model the behaviour and to let others know that the
same behaviour is allowed and expected in the team.

COACHING PRACTICE
Opening up and being honest
Choose a topic about which you have been reluctant to speak your mind.
Think through what you want to say to the team, and make sure that
your speaking will make a positive contribution rather than put someone
down. Say that you would like to speak openly and honestly about the
issue and that you're not attacking anyone, and then have your say. Ask
for feedback.

QUESTIONS AND OBSERVATIONS
• How was your speaking received?
• Were you able to read the reactions of people when you spoke?

- What are the benefits of speaking up?
- What are the risks of speaking up? Can you manage the risks?
- Can you hear feedback without becoming defensive? Can you listen generously to the feedback?

▶ COLLABORATION STRATEGY
Monitor how others respond

Noticing how others react to you is a useful skill to develop if you want to be a collaborative leader. It doesn't stop with just noticing. If you detect that someone is reacting in a negative way, either through their body language or something they said, pay attention to that because there is communication in that reaction. As a collaborative leader, this kind of response should trigger some action from you to investigate further.

Reading and listening to the emotions of others and responding is an important part of being collaborative. There is so much information contained in emotions, but often in the workplace there are unwritten rules about controlling your emotions. This dismisses a large part of what it is to be human and forces people to close themselves down. Paying attention to the emotional landscape doesn't mean you are becoming a therapist or counsellor, it simply means you are including the whole person in your interactions and this is one way to really engage with others in a positive and respectful way.

COACHING PRACTICE
Paying attention to reactions

When you notice someone reacting but saying nothing, choose the right moment to ask about that reaction. Investigate what caused it and listen generously in order to understand.

QUESTIONS AND OBSERVATIONS
- What did you learn?
- What was the benefit of this practice and what impact did you have?
- How can this approach benefit a collaborative style of leadership?

►COLLABORATION STRATEGY
Create the right environment

If you want to lead and develop strong engagement with business goals, create an environment where team members will speak up. You can encourage your team members to do this by acknowledging people who do speak up and by inviting others to have a say.

Even if you don't agree with what someone said, you can still openly appreciate their contribution, so that they are more likely to speak again. The collective wisdom in an organisation lives in its employees and we want to tap into that wisdom whenever we can. By doing that we arrive at better quality decisions.

It's very important to never belittle anyone for speaking up in a meeting. This sends entirely the wrong message and will undermine your efforts to encourage collaboration.

COACHING PRACTICE
Inviting others to speak up

Choose an appropriate moment and invite team members to speak up. You can explain that you value their opinions and their knowledge and would like them to contribute and speak up when they have something to add.

QUESTIONS AND OBSERVATIONS
- How did the team react to your encouragement?
- How can you continue to build trust and create an environment where team members feel comfortable speaking up?
- When team members speak up, how do you react? Can you allow this without becoming defensive?

►COLLABORATION STRATEGY
Ask team members to get things done

Are you making requests of others to get things done? Some people find making requests difficult because it puts someone on the spot. It also potentially puts you on the spot if they respond with a blunt no. Being collaborative requires embracing your discomfort, so accept that the response could be negative and ask anyway. Keep in mind that making requests more often than not leads to progress.

COACHING PRACTICE

Making requests

Think of certain requests that you have held yourself back from making for some reason. Maybe you forgot, or maybe you were concerned about how the person in question might react.

Go ahead and make the requests and ask for a completion date. This will turn the request into a commitment (more on this later, but without a commitment, nothing has really been agreed).

This can be challenging with someone you aren't used to making requests to. But don't be apologetic. You can explain why you need their support.

QUESTIONS AND OBSERVATIONS

• Did you find making these requests uncomfortable? If so, why?
• Why do you hold yourself back from making requests?
• Are certain people more difficult to make requests to than others? Why is that?

▶ COLLABORATION STRATEGY

Offer clear and honest assessments

How do you support your team members, your peers and the person you report to? Are you able to be open and honest with them about their work performance? Are you prepared to say what needs to be said to support them being successful? If not, then you are holding yourself back from working effectively. This needs to be addressed if you are committed to becoming a collaborative leader.

COACHING PRACTICE

Creating feedback opportunities

Identify someone with whom you are unable to be open and honest about their work performance. Plan a conversation with them with a view to giving each other feedback in a way that supports both of you.

This might be easier initially with someone who reports to you. Discuss how you can help each other to be more effective.

QUESTIONS AND OBSERVATIONS
• Can you see any patterns in the way you relate to people that prevent you having open, honest conversations that would provide feedback in a supportive way?
• Are there other relationships you have that would benefit from a conversation to open up the communication?

||||||||||||||||||||||||||||||||||||||||||||||||||||||||||||||||||||||||||||||||||||||||||||||||||||||||||||||||||||||||||||||||||||||||||||||||||||||||||||||||||||

PERSONAL EXPERIENCE

Speaking straight is a skill that I have worked at developing.

I was brought up in a family where the values were somewhat old-fashioned. My maternal grandfather was a police inspector who had been quite strict with my mother and her siblings. My father also had a strict upbringing and the message I took from my parents was that it wasn't okay to challenge people who are in a more senior position.

I was a young leader working in manufacturing in the late 1980s and 1990s, and I remember having strict rules about treating senior leaders as though they were always right. This was quite a childish view of the world and I've outgrown that now, to the point where I will speak up with anyone if I feel it's necessary.

The problem with not speaking up is that the organisation doesn't benefit from your wisdom. There were times in the past when I could have spoken up but chose not to, out of fear of reprisal or fear of making a mistake. There were times when I was disappointed in senior leaders because they weren't always treating others with dignity and respect. This affected me personally on a couple of occasions, and this is one of the reasons I teach and coach collaboration skills, because these values resonate very strongly with me.

I understand that for some people speaking straight can be risky. I suggest taking it slowly to begin with and starting with low-risk options, then building to addressing more challenging audiences as your confidence grows.

As a leader, encouraging and acknowledging straight speaking in your team and being careful not to put down anyone who speaks up will create a safe environment.

One of the managers I reported to, Paul, was particularly good at speaking straight and I learned a lot from him. He would give me direct feedback, which at times was very confronting. He was very skillful at pointing out areas where I had blind spots, and he did this in a way that was both challenging and supportive. He also pointed out opportunities for me to speak straight with others and he would check back with me to support me in doing that. It was as though he was giving me permission to speak up. As a result of his feedback I developed my ability to allow myself to be uncomfortable and speak straight with others.

I've also witnessed speaking straight done badly. This occurs more often when there is a lack of empathy between people. One person says something they think is helpful and the other person takes what was said the wrong way and reacts emotionally. The speaker doesn't realise they have been misunderstood because there isn't the trust in the relationship that allows them to perceive that fact. The speaker may then end up reacting to the other person's reaction. This is how silos begin to develop in organisations. Two people have a misunderstanding and don't clean that up afterwards.

More on that in the next chapter.

CHAPTER 4

Being for Each Other

Supporting each other's success. Operating from the point of view that team members are all in it together and that nobody can win at the expense of someone else or the business objectives. Looking for each other's greatness and providing rigorous support when needed.

How are you supporting others to succeed?

* * *

Being for each other is different from making case-by-case assessments of someone's actions and behaviours, and being for them or not depending on your judgments. Being for each other requires that you make a strong commitment to support other team members in *all* circumstances.

Being for someone doesn't mean that you will always agree with them, but it does mean you will speak straight when you don't agree with them. Supporting others in learning from their mistakes, rather than putting them down, and offering constructive criticism are ways to be for someone.

The internal workings of an organisation can become a battleground. Different departments defend themselves from perceived attack. People gossip about each other and deliberately undermine what others are trying to achieve. Competition is the rule, and sometimes not fair competition. In more extreme circumstances, colleagues become enemies, sabotaging each other's achievements and negatively influencing those around them.

Success in the marketplace can become a low priority in such a petty-minded environment.

►COLLABORATION STRATEGY
Choose to be for someone

Start by accepting others as they are and believing in them. Make a commitment to other people's successes and look for a positive intent in everything they do. In my experience, people who proceed with a negative intent are in a small minority.

It doesn't require that you like someone in order to be for them. In fact, being for someone who is a close friend can sometimes be more difficult than with a more distant work colleague. Giving frank, open insights to a close friend can challenge the friendship at times, and the stakes may seem higher.

COACHING PRACTICE
Offering support during setbacks

Look for recent or current situations where the outcome desired by a team member didn't eventuate. Explore the reasons for the result with them. Give them encouragement to keep going and offer your support if appropriate.

This may be something you do already; however, it can be a blind spot for some leaders.

The trick is to notice if the person is moving into defensiveness. If they are becoming defensive, ask them to tell you what their observations are, rather than you telling them yours. Focus on asking questions rather than making statements that could be construed as judgments.

QUESTIONS AND OBSERVATIONS

- How open are you to reviewing any errors you have made in the past?
- Are you willing to review your errors with your team so that everyone can learn?
- Can you think of any instances when the team didn't learn from a mistake? Can that be rectified now?

►COLLABORATION STRATEGY
Acknowledge effort rather than results

If you want to be for team members and give them encouragement, look for opportunities to acknowledge their efforts and not just results. The efforts we make are something we largely control; the results can be more variable, as a number of factors outside our control are usually involved. If team members are recognised for their efforts, they are more likely to make even greater efforts in the future.

COACHING PRACTICE
Recognising contributions
Look for examples where team members have put in a lot of effort, regardless of the result. Make a point of recognising this. The greatest effort is often made on days when the results are poorest. If team members are only used to being recognised for results, they might be surprised to have their efforts noticed.

QUESTIONS AND OBSERVATIONS
• How are team members reacting to this recognition of effort?
• What impact is this having on the team as a whole?
• If your team members have their own teams to manage, are they recognising the efforts being made?

▶ **COLLABORATION STRATEGY**
Explain to your team what it means to be for each other
Building a shared understanding of "being for each other" and the practices that support that approach will be a powerful step in developing a more collaborative culture.

COACHING PRACTICE
Creating guidelines
Encourage your team members to appreciate the potential benefits of being for each other. Ask them to imagine a team of people determined to be for each other compared to a team that isn't behaving that way. The power of the former is going to make that team so much more successful, plus the work environment will be much more pleasant. It's difficult to see a reason not to want to practise this approach.

You could pass on the following guidelines for being for each other:
1. Give each other encouragement.
2. Clean up any misunderstandings in a timely manner (more on this below).
3. Intervene when others are gossiping. Saying nothing when you hear gossip effectively condones it.
4. Stand up for others if someone puts them down.
5. Be open to constructive feedback from others.

QUESTIONS AND OBSERVATIONS
• How did the team react to the discussion on being for each other?
• Is there any history of not being for each other in the team? If so, can you discuss moving on from the past and becoming a supportive team?

▶ COLLABORATION STRATEGY
Resolve conflicts
One way to build a culture of being for each other is to resolve long-held grudges or conflicts that didn't end productively. In most cases this will have involved a difference of opinion and a lack of respect on the part of one or both parties involved. As mentioned in the last chapter, this is the way that unhealthy silos develop in businesses: a difference of opinion occurs and, to deal with the emotion they still feel, instead of working towards resolution, people find it easier to gossip about it.

It can be uncomfortable to do the hard work of conflict resolution. The following practice is about doing that hard work.

COACHING PRACTICE
Cleaning up disagreements
Think of someone with whom you have had a disagreement that didn't end on a positive note. This can be at work or outside work. Have a conversation to "clean up" that situation with the person. This might involve an apology or an explanation along with some good listening. If you can have this conversation without needing to claim that you are right or trying to defend yourself, it will nearly always have a better outcome. If the need to win is greater than the need to clean up, then the

outcome may be the same as before. Don't have the conversation if you feel you need to be victorious over the other person.

The more you practise these clean-up activities, the shorter the time will be between realising you need to do a clean-up and actually doing it. Eventually, you will start to realise while in the midst of a disagreement that listening, or a clean-up, is necessary and you will do it straightaway.

In most cases, a successful resolution of a grudge or difficult relationship will result in a lighter feeling and allow more energy to be channelled into positive action.

QUESTIONS AND OBSERVATIONS

- What was difficult about this conversation? Was it getting started? The feelings involved? The lingering desire to defend yourself?
- How did the conversation end?
- Is there a need to have a follow-up?
- Can you stop thinking about the issue now; in other words, is it truly resolved?

▶ COLLABORATION STRATEGY

Differentiate between collaboration and being liked

Some people mistake collaboration for liking others or needing to be liked. This is incorrect. It's possible to collaborate really well with someone you don't particularly like; you can still share a common purpose. It's also possible to collaborate very poorly or not at all with someone you like.

COACHING PRACTICE

Seeing opportunities for improvement

Think of the people you work with and give yourself marks out of ten for how well you work with each of them. Can you identify someone you work with but struggle to make progress with on business goals? Plan a strategy to improve this situation, perhaps using some of the practices in this book.

QUESTIONS AND OBSERVATIONS
- What is it about this relationship you have identified that doesn't promote good collaboration and progress?
- Is your strategy for improvement addressing this issue?

▶ **COLLABORATION STRATEGY**
Identify unfinished business
Have you had any conversations recently that you've thought about again more than twice since they occurred? What is it about the conversation that draws you back to it? In all likelihood there is some unfinished business left over from the discussion. Multiplied throughout an organisation, these little pieces of unfinished business can result in a slowing-down effect. The following practice focuses on undoing that unhealthy silo mentality.

COACHING PRACTICE
Reaching out to other departments
Think of someone in a different department with whom you aren't able to get on well. There may be some history between you; it may relate to specific comments made in the past, or it could just be their body language or the way they speak that puts you off. Have a conversation with that person to build bridges. Maybe compliment them in some way or talk about the past event that didn't go so well with the aim of cleaning that up.

QUESTIONS AND OBSERVATIONS
Review how the conversation went.
- Was there anything you learned from the conversation?
- Would you approach this kind of situation differently next time?
- Are there other people in the organisation with whom this sort of conversation would be relevant and potentially constructive?

▶ **COLLABORATION STRATEGY**
Create healthy silos
Returning to the subject of silos in organisations, is there such a thing

as a healthy or unhealthy silo? Human beings haven't lost all their tribal instincts and this is often very apparent in organisations. The trick is to have strong silos that collaborate with each other. This requires collaborative leaders who lead by example. Maintaining healthy relationships across silos requires a commitment from everyone to work together and resolve differences, and an awareness that gossip is destructive (more on this below).

COACHING PRACTICE
Auditing the silos in your business
Have a discussion with your team about the other departments that you interact with and review how well those interactions are going. Identify which aspects of the interdepartmental relationships are healthy and which are unhealthy. Make a plan to address the unhealthy relationships, while identifying some specific business outcomes as the desired result.

QUESTIONS AND OBSERVATIONS
• How did the team respond? The response will tell you how much work there is to do.
• Did you hear anything new in your team's views?
• How will you engage them in taking a collaborative approach?

▶ COLLABORATION STRATEGY
Challenge gossip
Nearly everyone has gossiped at some point, speaking about someone negatively with no intention of sharing the feedback with them. Who did you gossip about recently? What was your reason for gossiping?

When we gossip, it usually means there is some unfinished business that we are avoiding. Gossip destroys collaboration. It creates filters for people throughout the organisation that slow actions down. It also breeds distrust—after all, if I hear you gossiping about someone, what are you saying about me when I'm not present?

COACHING PRACTICE
Eliminating the need for gossip
Think of someone you gossiped about. What was the unfinished business underlying your gossip? Go and complete that unfinished business with the person concerned. This takes some courage. It might mean clearing up an unresolved conflict or delivering some feedback you have long wanted to give them. If you can do this in a positive way, there will no longer be any need to gossip about that person. It can also result in you letting go of some resentment you may have been holding on to.

QUESTIONS AND OBSERVATIONS
- Are there other people you have gossiped about with whom you have unfinished business to attend to?
- Can you make a commitment to stop gossiping?
- Can you role-model more positive behaviour and thereby inspire those around you to be more effective collaborators?

▶ COLLABORATION STRATEGY
Give yourself permission to be uncomfortable
If you want to develop your interpersonal skills and be a skillful collaborator, the self-development that occurs is usually accompanied by discomfort as you try out new approaches. Often our natural tendency is to avoid discomfort, so consciously permitting ourselves to experience discomfort makes sense.

COACHING PRACTICE
Embracing discomfort in order to be for someone
Can you think of someone you avoid at work? Make a decision to have a conversation with them about a work matter. In that conversation, make sure that you practise good listening. Thank them for something they said or contributed to the conversation.

QUESTIONS AND OBSERVATIONS
- How uncomfortable were you having this conversation?

- Are there similar conversations you could have with others in your organisation?
- Why do you avoid certain people (if you do)?

IIIIIIIIIIIIIIIIIIIIIIIIIIIIIIIIIIIIIIIIIIIIIIIIIIIIIIIIIIIIIIIIIIIIIIIIIIIIIIIIIIIIIIIIIIIIIIIIIIIIIIIIIIIIIIIIIIIIIIIIIIIIIIIIIIIIIIIIIIIIIIIIIIIIIIIIIIIIIIIIIIIIIIIIIIIIIIIIIIIII

PERSONAL EXPERIENCE

I've had some personal experience of environments where constant gossip and a lack of being for each other damaged teamwork.

The effects of gossip and undermining others results in a slowing-down effect on the achievement of business objectives. Team members become distracted from what's important, begin to focus on what isn't important (gossip) and then spend more time on this non-productive behaviour. This is especially hard to change when a leader indulges in gossip and thereby sets the example for everyone else. I've worked in organisations where different departments were virtually at war with each other. Such wars continue until someone in a leadership position says enough is enough and starts taking action to build bridges.

Adopting a listening approach and expressing a desire to work together for the benefit of the business is a good starting point. After that, listening generously to feedback on how you and your department have failed to collaborate, without becoming defensive, will nearly always contribute to an improved situation. Getting into a "we are right and you are wrong" conversation doesn't help build collaboration.

I once worked with a group of maintenance-team leaders and their new manager and they were in a very dark place when I started working with them. They had been through a forced redundancy program that had resulted in many of their colleagues departing the business. They were left with a much higher workload and were not feeling any appreciation from the leaders in the business for their efforts in coping with the change and the new workload.

I realised that to be for this team would require some listening at first. I estimated that three hours of listening would be sufficient; instead, three half-day sessions of listening were required for these experienced people to express their grief and dissatisfaction with the way they had been treated and with the changes that had occurred.

There was a noticeable shift in the energy and atmosphere once they had been heard out and understood. The fourth session was much more positive and in the last session the team were able to start focusing on each other and how they could be a better team and be for each other. They gave each other feedback in a one-on-one process.

If I had insisted on moving at my pace rather than theirs, we wouldn't have seen that shift happen. There would have been unfinished business.

This was an example of using generous listening, a little straight speaking and an attitude of being for team members in order to bring about a shift in team dynamics.

The manager of this team subsequently embraced the idea of collaboration and began devoting his time to building the right team culture. He was prepared to look at his own behaviour first and to change it, if necessary, to obtain the desired outcome. His commitment made all the difference.

How often do we see change management that doesn't allow time for team members to make the required emotional adjustment? Understanding change from a purely intellectual perspective can happen pretty much instantaneously; however, it can take much longer for processing to occur at an emotional level. Failing to act in a way that shows you are being for team members often does significant damage to those most affected by change. This can result in what I call "post-transformation stress disorder". The antidote to this is to create a collaborative culture before embarking on organisational change.

CHAPTER 5

Honouring Commitments

Making commitments that build towards agreed objectives. Being responsible for your commitments and holding others accountable for theirs. Supporting others in fulfilling their commitments.

Are you creating and managing commitments?

* * *

If you want to be an effective collaborative leader, then forging a culture where commitments are created and honoured will be high on your list of priorities. Once there is a common understanding and agreement that honouring commitments is a good idea for the purpose of delivering business results, then it will start to become reality.

This is an area where I see organisations consistently struggle. It's often because of a lack of clarity in people's minds about how commitments will be managed. Many leaders get incredibly frustrated and upset with team members because they "just will not honour their commitments". This can result in disciplinary action being taken and trust being eroded—all because there was no clarity in the first place from the leaders.

▶COLLABORATION STRATEGY
Make each commitment a relationship

If a commitment doesn't have someone clearly identified as the person responsible for carrying it out, together with a date by which the commitment will be completed, then there's nothing to honour. Effectively, there is no commitment. Most often it will result in no action and a frustrated team.

To make commitments more powerful, have them exist in a relationship. This means having commitments exist between two people, an owner and a receiver. The owner has to fulfil the commitment, and the receiver provides support, following up on the commitment and offering assistance to ensure it is completed on time, or renegotiating the commitment in the event of unexpected roadblocks.

COACHING PRACTICE
Implementing a relationship
Introduce the idea to your team of commitments existing in relationships. Review the commitments you have made in light of this and identify who is the owner of each commitment and who is the receiver. You may have to appoint receivers for specific commitments.

QUESTIONS AND OBSERVATIONS
• What challenges, if any, do you need to overcome to make this work?
• Is anyone resisting the idea of commitments having an owner and a receiver?
• What are the reasons for any resistance? Are commitments clearly prioritised for the team?

►COLLABORATION STRATEGY
Make sure everyone is performing at the same level
The first step in performance management is to clearly identify expectations and check that these are understood and agreed upon.

You will be aware of people in your organisation who are known for being great at honouring their commitments (you might be one of them). What are these people like?
1. They are very organised with their commitments.
2. They don't take on more than they can do.
3. They say no when they know they can't deliver.
4. They wear their commitments like a badge of honour.
5. Others trust them because they know they repeatedly do what they say.

Contrast this with people who are not good at honouring commitments:
1. They are very disorganised when it comes to commitments.

2. They often make the mistake of saying yes to everything and then getting very little done.
3. They are not seen as particularly trustworthy because people have come to regard them as someone they can't rely on.
4. They might have a reputation for being someone who talks a lot but doesn't do much.

When you have a situation where not everyone is pulling their weight, people who are honouring their commitments start to feel used and overworked because others go to them first, as they know they will get a result. If someone is regularly allowed to miss their commitments, a sense of unfairness can grow within the team. So it's essential to get everyone performing at a similar high level.

COACHING PRACTICE
Setting clear expectations
Meet your team members *individually* to discuss their commitments. When reviewing those commitments, identify what the priorities are and when each commitment is due to be completed. If any commitments have been missed, ensure that each one is discussed and a resolution reached.

In following up on broken commitments, discuss why the commitment is important and check that the person has the capability and support to complete the task. Then make a new commitment.

QUESTIONS AND OBSERVATIONS
• What action is required to ensure future commitments are kept?
• What were the consequences of any missed commitments? Have those been discussed with the person concerned?

▶ COLLABORATION STRATEGY
Lead by example
It's very important that you as a leader are role-modelling the right behaviour with regard to honouring commitments. To be in a leadership position and hold others accountable for their commitments requires that you are always managing yours.

COACHING PRACTICE
Monitoring your own commitments
Review the commitments that are "current" for you. How well
organised are your commitments? Do you have an effective structure
for monitoring what you have agreed to do? Who are your commitments
with?

   Examine your priorities. Are there any commitments you could
remove from the list or renegotiate so you can meet them? Are there any
commitments missing from your list?

QUESTIONS AND OBSERVATIONS
• How well organised are your commitments?
• What will it take for you to become adept at creating and honouring
  commitments?
• Can you become systematic about reviewing your commitments?

►COLLABORATION STRATEGY
Keep the team aligned
As discussed above, building a common understanding in the team about
a shared practice of honouring commitments is a powerful leadership
action, so it's worth making some extra effort to follow through on this
and underline the potential benefits. These will be numerous and include:
   1. Clarity of purpose amongst team members
   2. Action plans that are both realistic and get executed
   3. A supportive culture
   4. Business performance improvement
   5. Alignment on goals.

COACHING PRACTICE
Taking responsibility
Initiate a conversation with your team about the way that you all honour
commitments at the moment. What ways can you and the team see to
improve how you collectively do this?

   First, ask team members to look at the way they manage their own
commitments and then come back to discuss further. Can the team

members constructively criticise themselves and share their thoughts on how to improve? The best outcome is that team members take responsibility for looking at themselves first. That way, honouring commitments will soon become part of your team culture.

Also discuss how you can support each other in honouring commitments.

QUESTIONS AND OBSERVATIONS
• What are the biggest challenges in leading your team members into a consistent practice of honouring commitments?
• How can you support them to prioritise their actions so that honouring commitments becomes easier for them and also meets the needs of your business?

► COLLABORATION STRATEGY
Review team commitments regularly
To reinforce the work you have already done on aligning the team and helping them understand the importance of honouring commitments, make it a habit to get together regularly as a group and review your progress.

COACHING PRACTICE
Holding a team update
If you don't do this already, organise a regular meeting with the whole team to review each person's commitments. This should be a supportive meeting that helps everyone understand how each person on the team is progressing.

Discussing how team members can support each other will build collaboration. Some team members will be more focused when it comes to completing their commitments, and a team discussion should have the goal of helping others learn from them.

QUESTIONS AND OBSERVATIONS
• After your first few meetings, consider whether there are any team members who would benefit from another one-on-one discussion about

their commitments. Can you identify those who are finding it difficult to stay focused?

- What would you say to those people in a private discussion? (Hint: generous listening, speaking straight and being for each other all apply.)

►COLLABORATION STRATEGY
Be open about broken commitments

Creating and maintaining a team culture of honouring commitments will involve having open discussions about broken commitments. These conversations need to encompass acknowledgment of what has happened, a review of why it happened and a decision on next steps, including renewing the commitment if appropriate.

It should be made clear that missing commitments doesn't mean you aren't honouring them. Sometimes, external factors, such as a change in priorities, will make it impossible for a commitment to be met. If you are aware of the change and take action to renegotiate the timeline, then you are still taking responsibility for your commitment.

COACHING PRACTICE
Admitting to your own failures

Identify any commitments you have missed recently and discuss these with the team. Let everyone know that you are taking responsibility for the missed commitment and that you are making another commitment that you intend to keep. Ask a team member to work with you and support you to keep the commitment.

By taking this action you are role-modelling the practice of honouring commitments.

QUESTIONS AND OBSERVATIONS

- How did the team react to your role-modelling?
- How easy was it for you to admit a shortfall on your part?
- What are the benefits of being open and honest about this?

► **COLLABORATION STRATEGY**

Make it clear it's okay to say no

Does your team have a "can-do" approach to commitments? Sometimes this results in team members saying yes to everything, even when it's not possible for them to meet all their commitments. This might be because they feel uncomfortable saying no.

It's much better to hear a request declined than get a yes that results in a no later, when the deadline has passed. Giving team members permission to decline a request, or to negotiate the completion date, helps them to manage their goals. This will increase the likelihood that commitments that are made are subsequently honoured. Allowing for a no makes room for a more emphatic yes.

COACHING PRACTICE

Declining wisely

Have a conversation with the team about managing commitments. Explain that they are responsible for managing their commitments, including rescheduling and declining requests. Advise them that when they decline a commitment they should explain that it is because their priorities mean they are unable to meet the request. If they can see other ways of completing the task, such as someone else taking on the commitment, then they should propose those options.

QUESTIONS AND OBSERVATIONS

- Have you become aware of any team members who say yes to commitments all the time and then fail to deliver?
- How can you support these team members to be more effective at managing their commitments?
- What conversations do you need to have to help them see the gap in their performance?

||||||||||||||||||||||||||||||||||||||||||||||||||||||||||||||||||||||||||||||||||||||||||||||||||||||||||||||||||||||||||||||||||||||||||||||||||

PERSONAL EXPERIENCE

I've noticed how good I feel when I keep my commitments. It's because I get a sense of satisfaction from having achieved something.

When I'm clear about what I want to achieve—for example, writing this book—and I take action on a daily basis to make progress, I feel good about myself and this builds momentum. If I miss a commitment, for whatever reason, I don't feel so good; but this just drives me to do better next time, especially if I have let someone else down.

Acknowledging when commitments are kept, and celebrating them, is a good way to build a team practice of honouring commitments. The positive experience will make team members come back for more!

A simple example of where most of us make and keep commitments is in our relationships with those closest to us. Every day we make and keep commitments, such as cooking a meal, taking our children to school, going to work, taking children to sporting activities—the list goes on. We take these commitments for granted and we mostly enjoy serving and supporting our family members.

Bringing this same level of commitment into the workplace will have a powerful effect. When commitments are linked to team goals, what you are doing makes more sense and the motivation to honour commitments grows. And when everyone in the team is committed to the same goals, the momentum and motivation of the team builds, and honouring commitments becomes the norm.

This is when work becomes very rewarding and the team can be defined as high-performing.

CHAPTER 6

Acknowledgment and Appreciation

**Making a commitment to be a source of acknowledgment
and appreciation for the team. This includes giving, receiving
and requesting acknowledgment.**

Are you a source of acknowledgment and appreciation?

* * *

The practice of acknowledgment and appreciation is a skill that can be
learned and used as a powerful tool for collaboration. It will require just a
few minutes of your time each day, but will have a significant impact on
individuals you work with.

Consider the difference between being acknowledged and appreciated
and being taken for granted. Acknowledging and appreciating someone
for their effort can lift that person's performance, motivation and
enthusiasm for a long time. This in turn can positively affect the person's
colleagues, as they will find they are now working with someone who is
more motivated. Thus, the practice of acknowledgment and appreciation,
if done skilfully, can influence many people—and create a more
enjoyable workplace.

▶ **COLLABORATION STRATEGY**

Use acknowledgment and appreciation effectively

Practising acknowledgment and appreciation skilfully involves more
than occasionally saying "good job". It is actually a skill that can be
developed over time and help you have a much greater impact on others.

What are the components of good acknowledgment and appreciation?
Here are some questions to consider when preparing to acknowledge
someone:

1. What, specifically has the person done? Can you describe what they did and the effort that was involved?
2. What were the circumstances around the person's achievement? Describing these will demonstrate that you have a good understanding of what the person has been doing and this will contribute to the impact of your acknowledgment.
3. What was the impact on you of what the person did? Describe this in some detail: how you felt, and what changed in or for you as a result of their efforts.
4. What impact has this person had on the future of the company? Will their efforts lead to any changes in your plans or the company's direction?

It isn't necessary to cover all of this in every acknowledgment. The purpose here is to stimulate some thinking about how to make your acknowledgments more powerful.

COACHING PRACTICE

Planning and delivering acknowledgment and appreciation
Identify something about each of your team members that you could acknowledge and appreciate. Can you use the list above to describe in detail what each team member has achieved recently?

Have you already acknowledged each individual personally for their identified achievement? If not, take the time to do so.

QUESTIONS AND OBSERVATIONS
• How did each person react to your acknowledgment?
• Are your team members used to receiving acknowledgment and appreciation from you?
• Is it necessary to explain that you are now focusing more on this as a practice and that receiving it is also a skill?

▶ COLLABORATION STRATEGY

Make acknowledgment and appreciation a conscious practice
Making acknowledgment and appreciation part of your daily routine is necessary if you want to develop a culture where this practice

becomes normal behaviour. If you aren't doing this, it's unlikely that your team will be.

The key is to make the practice authentic. Avoid acknowledging others just for the sake of it. If you give acknowledgment that isn't authentic, people will usually realise this and it will cost you some credibility.

If you can't be authentic, find out more about the circumstances of each achievement before practising acknowledgment.

COACHING PRACTICE
Building an aligned approach
Initiate a conversation about the practice of acknowledgment and appreciation with your team. The purpose of this conversation is to find out what their views are on the subject.

If you already have a regular practice of acknowledgment and appreciation, then the conversation will serve to bring this subject into sharper focus. If the practice is not part of the team culture, then the conversation can serve to develop the idea of including it.

QUESTIONS AND OBSERVATIONS
- What are the next steps for you and your team in developing a culture of acknowledgment and appreciation?
- What resistance is there in the team to this practice?
- Are there individuals who don't like the idea? What are their reasons for being resistant?

►COLLABORATION STRATEGY
Assess why you may not give acknowledgment and appreciation
Here are some reasons and beliefs people use to explain why they don't routinely give acknowledgment and appreciation:
1. Team members are just doing their job. That doesn't require acknowledgment. (Is that true? Aren't people who turn up every day making a consistent effort worthy of acknowledgment?)
2. People might slow down and relax if I acknowledge them. (Actually, the opposite is probably true.)

3. It's not the normal behaviour in this organisation. (Well, you can be the first to start it.)
4. It's risky because the person might reject my acknowledgment. (If they do reject it then you can talk about the skill of accepting acknowledgment and how that affects the team culture overall.)
5. I don't want the person to know I admire something they did. (Ask yourself why that is the case.)
6. It's a waste of time. (Do you like to be acknowledged? Do you think others like to be acknowledged?)
7. It's risky because I might not appear authentic. (In that case, make sure you understand the details of what you are acknowledging the person for and ask their work colleagues what they did that was worth acknowledging.)
8. Others may resent someone else being acknowledged. (Be clear what it is about this person's effort that has attracted the acknowledgment. Resentment isn't a reason to stop acknowledging.)

As you can see, the benefits of acknowledging others far outweigh any potential downside.

COACHING PRACTICE
Identifying team members you neglect
Can you think of anyone who you have avoided acknowledging in the past? What were your reasons for doing that? Was there some disagreement that meant you had unfinished business with that person?

Are you competing with someone and you don't want them to know you admire something they did? Or did someone reject your acknowledgment in the past and that put you off trying again?

If it's clear you have avoided acknowledging someone, then you aren't being for that person and action is required to clean up that relationship. Take the time to have a discussion with the person in order to appreciate what they have achieved.

QUESTIONS AND OBSERVATIONS
• Can you see how your beliefs and stories about others can get in the way of acknowledging and appreciating them?

- Are there any other relationships where you consider acknowledgment and appreciation to be impossible or highly unlikely?
- Are you willing to address those relationships in order to improve collaboration?

▶ COLLABORATION STRATEGY
Show how to accept acknowledgment

Many people find it easier to give acknowledgment than to receive it. If you are one of those people, it is important to show how to accept acknowledgment. A simple "thank you" is often all that's required. The person giving you acknowledgment will feel great to hear you accept what they have said.

Creating a culture of acknowledgment and appreciation requires everyone to take responsibility for giving *and* receiving.

COACHING PRACTICE
Challenging rejection

If you notice someone not accepting acknowledgment, or deflecting it, challenge them and ask why they won't accept the compliment. Say that you understand it can be difficult to accept acknowledgment if we aren't used to it.

It may also be beneficial to talk about the bigger picture—the benefits of a workplace where people feel appreciated for their efforts and how, if everyone takes this approach, coming to work might become more enjoyable.

There will always be people who are cynical about acknowledgment and appreciation. Asking them why they take that view will encourage them to think about it.

QUESTIONS AND OBSERVATIONS
- How do you react to others acknowledging and appreciating you? Can you become a role model by graciously accepting appreciation?
- How do others react when you acknowledge them?
- Can you see how rejecting acknowledgment will reduce the likelihood of it becoming part of the workplace culture?

CHAPTER 7

Practising Inclusion

Always thinking about whether you are including all stakeholders in meetings, projects and decision-making. Being discerning about who to include and who not to include at various times. Communicating your thoughts about inclusion.

When did you last consciously practise inclusion and deliberately invite someone to a meeting for the purpose of including them?

* * *

When inclusion is practised skilfully, everyone will start to take ownership of outcomes because they are engaged.

The leader who commits to a practice of inclusion will be seen as a collaborative, participative leader. It's easy to follow a leader who takes this approach because, as a result of this kind of leadership, people will feel like they belong in the organisation. Contrast this with the way people are likely to feel alienated if they are not included.

If you hear the comment "Nobody told me", the chances are that the practice of inclusion was missing somewhere. These off-the-cuff remarks are worth paying attention to, as they are small signals of something important and potentially damaging going on in an organisation.

Getting inclusion right brings many benefits.

► **COLLABORATION STRATEGY**
Understand the benefits of inclusion
Including the right people at the right time in conversation will:
1. Ensure that their engagement with whatever is occurring is much more likely
2. Allow them to have input on a matter
3. Build alignment with a task or project

4. Increase the likelihood of wider organisational buy-in, as they will talk positively about their involvement
5. Increase motivation and engagement in general
6. Improve the quality of decisions, since more perspectives will be taken into consideration.

If, on the other hand, you fail to include the right people in a conversation, the following become risks:

1. People feel excluded and start to speak negatively about that with others; this, in turn, creates resistance to the development and success of a project.
2. People start to concoct and believe stories about a project; they might also create filters, such as "That will never succeed", "I can't support that because I had no input" or "They don't know what they're doing."
3. People are less likely to engage in future projects if they have felt excluded in the past.

COACHING PRACTICE

Getting your team aligned on inclusion

Discuss with your team the practice of inclusion. Use the points above to facilitate the discussion. Ask team members for examples of beneficial inclusion and of a failure to include. Quiz them about the benefits of inclusion and the downside of excluding people.

Review the last six months and consider where you could have been more effective in your practice of inclusion.

QUESTIONS AND OBSERVATIONS

- Do your team members see the benefits of practising inclusion?
- Can you and the team identify opportunities to consciously practise inclusion over the next few months?
- Are there any clean-ups you need to do in this area to let people know that you should have included them?
- Are there any examples of you over-including people and perhaps wasting their time?

► COLLABORATION STRATEGY

Make attendance optional

Another remark that is sometimes heard is, "Why am I in this meeting?" In some organisations, meetings seem to take over people's lives and the comment "I never get anything done because I'm always in meetings" is a frequent refrain.

It is possible to overdo inclusion. Sometimes, letting attendance at meetings be optional will be appropriate and beneficial. It still demonstrates inclusion, while also showing respect for team members' time constraints.

COACHING PRACTICE

Reviewing meeting invitations

Take a look at the lists of attendees for regular meetings and consider on a case-by-case basis whether they all need to be there. Then, where appropriate, give individuals the option to attend or not, as they see fit. Explain to each person that while you want to be inclusive, you don't want to waste anyone's valuable time unnecessarily. Say that if they choose not to attend you will still send them the meeting minutes. This should help you avoid any misunderstandings.

QUESTIONS AND OBSERVATIONS

- When you review meeting attendance, is there a case for discussing this with more senior people in your organisation?
- Can you see that time is wasted for some people at certain meetings?
- Could some people attend for the parts that concern them and leave for others?

► COLLABORATION STRATEGY

Ask for feedback on inclusion

Making your thinking explicit about inclusion leaves less room for misunderstanding. If you explain the reasons why you have invited some people to a discussion and not others, this will help clear up everyone's thinking. But it's also a good idea to ask meeting attendees if they think anyone you may have overlooked should be included, as it enables them to challenge your practice and provides important feedback.

COACHING PRACTICE

Making inclusion second nature

Make a habit of asking people about inclusion, especially at key moments, such as when decisions are going to be taken, new projects started or important announcements made.

QUESTIONS AND OBSERVATIONS

• How do you decide who should be included?
• Do you include people who wouldn't normally attend in some discussions to provide fresh perspectives?
• Would you invite someone from another department to your team meetings to offer new ideas and feedback on how you run your meetings?

►COLLABORATION STRATEGY

Say when you feel excluded

If you are going to role-model inclusion as a practice, this will mean speaking up when you feel you have been excluded. If you don't do this, you are effectively saying inclusion isn't that important, and you increase the risk of starting to feel some resentment yourself about being excluded. Letting others know you are interested and want to be included is a strong statement of a desire to collaborate and make a contribution.

COACHING PRACTICE

Voicing your concerns

Think of any recent situations where you felt excluded from something that you believed you should have been part of. Make a point of speaking with the person in charge and say that you would like to know why you were excluded, as you believe you might have had a contribution to make.

QUESTIONS AND OBSERVATIONS
• How was your speaking up received? Was it necessary to explain why you were making the point about inclusion?
• How can you avoid being excluded next time?
• Do you believe that your organisation is getting inclusion right most of the time? If not, where are there opportunities to improve?

▶ **COLLABORATION STRATEGY**

Review inclusion in decision-making

When making decisions, it's important to consider who needs to be involved and at what stage, and to make this a conscious process.

Next time you are about to make a major decision, ask yourself the following questions:
1. Who will take part in making the decision?
2. Who could help you make a better decision?
3. Who will be involved in the outcome of the decision?
4. Who would you like to engage and be part of the decision?
5. Who needs to be informed about the decision before it's made?
6. Who should be told about the decision once it has been made?

If you answer all these questions, the quality of the decision and consequent team alignment with the decision will most likely be high.

COACHING PRACTICE

Improving the quality of your next decision

Answer the questions above, then invite the people concerned to the next decision-making discussion. Let them know why you have invited them. Communicate any decisions made afterwards to those who need to be included.

QUESTIONS AND OBSERVATIONS
• How are people responding to being included in decision-making?
• Do you need to coach anyone on how to contribute more effectively to the decision-making process?
• Do you need to explain to anyone why they have been excluded from a process at any stage?

CHAPTER 8

Building Alignment

Taking action to ensure that all concerned parties are
supporting any particular decision as though they had made the
decision themselves. Allowing time for different perspectives to be
heard. Explaining the reasoning behind decisions that have been
made. Asking others to support decisions.

**Are you considering whether your actions are building alignment
with the direction you want to take as a leader?**

* * *

The main reason for practising listening generously, speaking straight, being for each other, honouring commitments, acknowledgment and appreciation, and inclusion is to continually build and maintain alignment across your team and the wider business.

These practices, if done consistently, will result in people becoming naturally aligned; moreover, these tools allow course corrections to be made if ever alignment is lost.

Allowing room for disagreements to occur is part of building alignment in a team. When handled sensitively, disagreements can be part of making the best decisions and be part of the process of inclusion. You want people to listen, but you also want them to speak up and have their say. When people are allowed to have their say and be heard on an issue, alignment naturally occurs.

When a leader uses the collaborative approaches described in this book, the team will support the decisions that are made because they will understand the reasoning behind them and they have been included in the process. And that will be the case even if not everyone agrees with the final outcome.

►**COLLABORATION STRATEGY**

Slow down to build alignment

In some circumstances, slowing a process down may increase collaboration. Some people think and talk quickly, not realising that they are leaving people behind. On top of that, if they show frustration with people who don't keep up, this discourages team members from asking for clarification.

COACHING PRACTICE

Moving at the right pace

When you are working on an important topic with others and alignment is desirable, slow down your speaking and the pace at which you are leading. Check regularly that team members are following what you are saying or proposing. Ask individuals to explain their understanding of the process, as a way of checking for alignment.

QUESTIONS AND OBSERVATIONS

- When you slow down, what do you say to yourself? What is your internal dialogue?
- What are the benefits of slowing down?
- What is the cost of slowing down?

►**COLLABORATION STRATEGY**

Allow team members to learn collaboration

If you give your team permission to gradually learn the skill of collaboration and treat it like a continuous improvement project, then your team members are more likely to commit to finding ways to co-operate. Collaboration is about working together to achieve common aligned goals. This requires conversations on a regular basis to update the alignment of the team.

If you make "the way we work together" as well as "what we do together" part of team discussions, it will significantly increase the chances of success. Teams that do this are in a small minority, so just by having that conversation, you will already be ahead of most of your competition.

COACHING PRACTICE
Checking in with your team
As a leader, make sure that the way you work together is a regular topic of discussion. This gives everyone permission to open up about what's not working for them. If you do this correctly, the team members will respond and have conversations that will in turn ensure they remain aligned.

At team meetings, ask if there are any issues with the way the group is working together. Make this a regular question, so that any issues are flushed out early, before they become more problematic.

This practice is a way to shape the culture of your team and maintain alignment on an ongoing basis.

QUESTIONS AND OBSERVATIONS
- Ask yourself, "How can I improve the conversation on the way we work together?"
- Is there anything you are doing that is impacting on the team being aligned?
- How will you ensure that your team is maintaining alignment with the company leadership and direction?
- What structure have you or can you create to ensure these alignment discussions occur regularly?

▶ COLLABORATION STRATEGY
Be alert for any lack of alignment
If you want to be a collaborative leader, it's necessary to be sensitive to whenever alignment within the team is missing. Obvious signs of this include team members gossiping, people complaining about other people and people complaining about other departments. Likewise, when someone is clearly trying to score points at someone else's expense, what you have is unhealthy competition rather than healthy collaboration.

If alignment is missing, it may be because the views of some people have not been heard and taken into account. In a collaborative team, it is expected that people will speak up when they aren't aligned. Therefore, make that expectation clear.

Sometimes the intractable problems are the ones that are avoided because the idea of entering into open conflict doesn't sit easily with some of the team. Instead the issues are discussed in corridors or behind closed doors and don't get resolved. This clearly doesn't build alignment; however, these difficult problems are exactly the sorts of issues that a collaborative approach will tackle.

COACHING PRACTICE
Requesting alignment
Are you aware of any areas where alignment is missing on a course of action? If so, have a conversation to build alignment. Sometimes emotions and conflicts can arise, especially with regard to subjects that have been avoided in the past.

If there is an intention and commitment to reach alignment at the outset from all participants, then the discussion will usually go well, in spite of any conflict. So asking for this commitment at the beginning of the discussion is a good first move.

QUESTIONS AND OBSERVATIONS
• If there is a lack of alignment, can you say why this hasn't been tackled before? Is it due to conflict aversion or another reason?
• Are any team members undermining alignment?
• If so, what action do you need to take to remedy this?

▶ COLLABORATION STRATEGY
Lead up
One of the ways to role-model leadership and collaboration in an organisation is to lead up. That simply means practising the skills of collaboration with more senior people.

If you speak straight with people more senior than you while being for them, they will usually appreciate your input. It will demonstrate that you care for them and the organisation.

Examples include speaking up when you are not aligned with a decision that has been made, making requests to senior staff for support and commitments to take specific actions, and perhaps even asking your manager to recognise someone who has made a significant contribution.

Some of the reasons or excuses for not leading up include:

1. It's not my place to challenge more senior people.
2. It could be a career-limiting step and be seen as disrespectful.
3. I might make a fool of myself.
4. My manager might react negatively.
5. My manager won't listen.

If you see that a senior person is making a mistake, is it better to say nothing or is it better to speak up for their and the organisation's benefit, even if it might make you uncomfortable?

COACHING PRACTICE

Speaking up to support your organisation

Can you think of an example of a time when you didn't speak up with your manager and this led to negative consequences?

When you encounter opportunities to lead up, stop and consider what you could say to help the situation. Also consider the best setting in which to have that conversation—probably not with an audience but rather in a one-on-one meeting.

QUESTIONS AND OBSERVATIONS

• What reasons, if any, do you have for not leading up?
• How are you censuring yourself at work? What are you not saying that you would like to say that would support your manager and the success of your business?

CHAPTER 9

Lines of Development

Understanding the ways in which you and others develop skills or intelligence in particular areas, or lines of development. Using this knowledge to analyse your and others' needs and to help sharpen your skills and those of your team.

How committed are you to your own development as a leader? How much time are you prepared to invest in yourself and others?

* * *

The term "lines of development" was used by Ken Wilber in his book *Integral Spirituality* (Integral Books, 2006) to describe the different skills or kinds of intelligence that a human being possesses and develops during a lifetime. Wilber postulated over a dozen different lines of development; here is a list of the major ones, along with their accompanying life questions.

LINE	*Life question*
COGNITIVE	*What am I aware of?*
SELF	*Who am I?*
VALUES	*What is significant to me?*
MORAL	*What should I do?*
INTERPERSONAL	*How should we interact?*
SPIRITUAL	*What is of ultimate concern?*
NEEDS	*What do I need?*
KINAESTHETIC	*How should I physically do this?*
EMOTIONAL	*How do I feel about this?*
AESTHETIC	*What is attractive to me?*

The lines I will refer to in relation to becoming a collaborative leader are the cognitive, emotional and interpersonal lines of development. The reason that these lines are important is that they are directly related to the development of the skills already described. The collaboration strategies that follow will show you how to assess and develop these particular lines and in turn make you and others more collaborative.

Cognitive line of development

This line describes a person's ability to understand multiple perspectives. Most people have had the experience of working with a leader who doesn't have great listening skills and makes a lot of decisions without referring to anyone else. This can reflect a low level of capability on the cognitive line. The "my way or the highway" approach to leadership doesn't usually result in a highly motivated and engaged team.

In contrast, the leader who usually asks for and considers the perspectives of others in the team tends to engage team members and create a sense of inclusion. This is an example of being more developed on the cognitive line.

▶ **COLLABORATION STRATEGY**

Develop your cognitive line to resolve conflict

Whenever you have difficulty or an emotional disagreement with another person, it's often because you haven't understood their point of view and they haven't understood yours.

COACHING PRACTICE

Improving your understanding of others

Think of a recent example where you disagreed with someone. What was their point of view? Can you describe their beliefs, feelings and understanding at the time of the disagreement?

This isn't about forcing agreement, but making an effort to understand another perspective. You might still disagree. If you didn't understand the other person's perspective, try and figure it out now. Better still, return to the conversation and ask them to explain their feelings and point of view, making sure you listen and don't get defensive.

Check that you have understood them correctly and then decide if your point of view has been modified. This quality of interaction tends to remove any heat from a dispute and amicable respect for each other's point of view can ensue.

QUESTIONS AND OBSERVATIONS
- Can you identify other areas where you have had unresolved disagreements? What do you think the other perspectives were that you didn't hear at the time?
- Are there people with whom you often disagree? Can you try to see their perspective? How do they view the issue in question?

► COLLABORATION STRATEGY
Develop your cognitive line to build engagement and ownership
When you are leading a team meeting or a project meeting, think about the different perspectives available in the room. Remember that the collective intellectual horsepower will almost certainly be much greater than the intelligence of any single individual.

With this in mind, ensure that everyone is given the opportunity to express their opinion. This might mean asking people to speak up. Some participants, especially the introverts in the room, may be reluctant to share their views. Nevertheless, ask the quiet attendees to say what they think.

There are many benefits to taking this approach:
1. You develop your cognitive line of development by listening to and understanding multiple perspectives.
2. The decision quality goes up because of the inclusion of different perspectives and the value they bring.
3. Team members feel included and valued, which builds trust, engagement and motivation.
4. People will feel more inclined to contribute again in the future if they have already been heard and valued.
5. The people in the meeting experience listening to multiple perspectives, which influences their cognitive line of development too.

COACHING PRACTICE
Asking for points of view
At your next team meeting, make it a specific goal to openly ask for contributions from the attendees. Don't be afraid to ask people their thoughts, to put them on the spot. If team members aren't accustomed to being asked for their contributions, there will be some uncomfortable silences. Allow these to happen. Those that aren't panicking will be thinking about what they are going to say.

At the end of the meeting, thank everyone for their input, mentioning some of the benefits you get when they speak up.

QUESTIONS AND OBSERVATIONS
- Can you see the value of uncomfortable silence?
- Did you notice any impact on meeting attendees when you were persistently asking for their contributions?
- Was there any discomfort for you? If you are used to running meetings where you do most of the talking, this practice may feel like a new move and potentially uncomfortable.
- What value did you see in the contributions from others?

Emotional line of development
The emotional line of development concerns our understanding of emotion and our capacity to be *with* strong emotions in others and ourselves. It's also about our ability to use language to describe emotions and the information contained in them.

How do you view your emotions and those of others? Do you embrace the emotional landscape as an integral part of your life?

Developing the emotional line cannot occur unless the cognitive line develops as well. If you can see only your perspective, in most cases you will either react emotionally to the perspectives of other people or dismiss them. If someone else is emotional about something, you will either become emotional too or shut their emotions down.

When you start to allow for multiple perspectives, sometimes those perspectives are accompanied by an emotional component, say anger or frustration. The more you practice accepting your emotions and those of others, without being overwhelmed by either, the more emotionally intelligent you become and the more your effectiveness as a leader increases.

When an emotional response occurs in you or in someone else, you can choose to remain rational. This can be a challenging moment; however, this is precisely when development occurs.

►COLLABORATION STRATEGY
Explore the emotional landscape

Deliberately observing and acknowledging the emotional landscape around you is one way to build awareness and become more skilled at recognising and managing emotions.

Have you heard the phrase "you should leave your emotions at the door when you come to work?" Does that make sense? It means you are being asked to ignore an incredibly important part of your being. And for what reason? Emotions are useful. After all, we want passion and desire to be expressed in the workplace too.

COACHING PRACTICE
Reviewing emotions

Take ten minutes at the end of each day for a period of a week to consider and make a note of the emotions you experienced yourself and the emotions you witnessed in others during that day.

QUESTIONS AND OBSERVATIONS
- Can you name all the emotions you witnessed? How did you react to the emotions you experienced?
- What information was contained in those emotions? How could that information be used constructively?

►COLLABORATION STRATEGY
Become more "present" to your emotions

One of the ways to develop on the emotional line is to acknowledge when you have reacted in an emotional way. Once you have come back to a calmer state, it might be appropriate to apologise, or provide an explanation of why you reacted the way you did. The key is to shorten the time between emotional interactions and cleaning up afterwards. Eventually, as you continue to manage your emotions and any fallout, you start to manage the emotion as it happens, and thereby avoid leaving any unfinished business.

Sometimes it is in our home life where emotions are more freely expressed, and this is fertile ground for working on your self-development.

COACHING PRACTICE
Achieving a positive outcome
Whenever you have an emotional interaction with anyone, take responsibility for reaching a positive outcome. This is really important to avoid any resentment, which can in turn have all sorts of negative and sometimes unseen consequences. Something to think about is whether it's better to be right and win, or work towards alignment with members of your team.

So, after any emotional interaction, stay with it until a satisfactory outcome is achieved. Don't give up. If the feelings are intense, come back later to resolve the issue.

QUESTIONS AND OBSERVATIONS
• What was the cause of the reaction? What was the thinking that created the emotional response?
• What did your emotions tell you at the time? Can you describe the emotions you experienced? Can you put this into words?
• How many perspectives were you considering when you had the emotional response? Did you clearly understand other perspectives around this issue?
• Are there specific individuals, at work or outside work, to whom you tend to respond in an emotional way?
• Can you see how listening to their perspectives and understanding those views will benefit both of you?

PERSONAL EXPERIENCE

When I was a team leader in my twenties, I had limited development on the emotional line. The way that manifested itself was in a fear of my emotions and a feeling that I needed to control them—the British stiff upper lip, if you like. I had internalised the message that it was bad to show emotions.

That didn't mean they went away. On the contrary, they seemed to intensify, so I was probably quite a serious young leader and not that easy to work with. I also ended up carrying all my unexpressed emotions around, which wasn't healthy. The way to remedy this was to grow on the emotional line and start expressing my emotions in a constructive way. A life's work!

In contrast, I dealt with leaders who "let it all hang out", so to speak, and expressed their emotions sometimes inappropriately and destructively, with little or no regard for the impact they had on others. Often they didn't even consider the impact, as they simply believed their way was the right way to lead. I witnessed several senior leaders expressing anger at individuals in a humiliating way, and this was something that I found unprofessional.

By focusing on self-development and working with various coaches throughout my career, I have developed my emotional line. I am now much more relaxed about my emotions and those of others.

Emotions contain a lot of information. When I have, or someone else has, an emotional response, I try to ask myself, "what is the information being communicated?" This approach gets underneath the emotion and looks for the message. Allowing the emotions to be and addressing the information they convey in a rational way is the goal.

The best place to practise is in close personal relationships. I've found this area has offered plentiful opportunities for me to grow by learning how not to react emotionally at times of conflict and instead seek to understand the information being communicated.

Interpersonal line of development

Conversations are such an integral part of leadership, and this line of development is all about our ability to use conversations in an effective, productive, impactful and inspiring way.

By now, you should be able to appreciate how the cognitive, emotional and interpersonal lines are related. If you are able to see multiple perspectives and embrace the presence of emotions in others, and yourself, conversations start to be an opportunity to work with others to create all sorts of inspiring possibilities. To take this further, practise the collaborative skills described in this book and think about the growth challenges in the cognitive and emotional lines. If you do this, your development on the interpersonal line is assured.

▶ **COLLABORATION STRATEGY**

Make the most of every conversation

Start to think of conversations as opportunities to engage, motivate, inspire and create. By embracing the practices in this book—listening generously, speaking straight, being for each other, creating and honouring commitments, offering acknowledgment and appreciation, and trying to build alignment—you will start to grow very quickly on the interpersonal line.

COACHING PRACTICE

Monitoring your interpersonal skills

Choose three key meetings each week where you will pay particular attention to your interpersonal skills. Try to include one or more meetings where you are leading.

QUESTIONS AND OBSERVATIONS

- What impact are you having on others in these meetings?
- What do you think attendees are saying after the meetings?
- Can you obtain feedback from one or two attendees? Ask them what they thought of the meeting and how it could be improved.

► **COLLABORATION STRATEGY**

Make constructive use of non-verbal communication

Think about intentionally using your body language and eye contact to demonstrate your interest and engagement. This can have a powerful impact on others during a conversation. Turning towards people you are speaking to, making frequent eye contact, nodding to show you are interested and listening, and smiling if you agree are all ways of being constructive. When relationship foundations are built in this way, disagreements can occur on safe, solid ground.

COACHING PRACTICE

Meeting people for the first time

When you meet people for the first time, make a point of using your body language in this constructive way. First impressions are important and making the effort on these occasions starts the relationship off on a good footing.

QUESTIONS AND OBSERVATIONS

• Can you see people respond to your non-verbal communication?
• What do you notice about the impact of other people's non-verbal communication on you?

► **COLLABORATION STRATEGY**

Review your conversations

You could apply the interpersonal line lens to each conversation you have. For example, after a conversation, ask yourself if you left feeling inspired, just okay or demotivated? These feelings tell you where that conversation was situated on the interpersonal line.

Thinking about how you are contributing to conversations and what impact you are having is a way of giving yourself feedback and taking responsibility for the way the conversation goes. The power of listening needs to be included here as a consideration. Most of us work out what we are thinking through dialogue or by writing. Being a great listener allows others to describe clearly what they are thinking. In this way, listening can be a practice to inspire others.

Monitoring your reaction

Notice how you feel after conversations in which you have participated. This is great feedback about the tone of the conversation. If you feel demotivated, can you identify what was missing from the conversation? Make some journal notes about conversations you have had each day and how they could have been more effective.

QUESTIONS AND OBSERVATIONS
- How are you contributing to the outcome of conversations you have?
- What could you do to improve the outcome of conversations, both in the way you feel afterwards and how clear the next steps are as a result of that discussion?

▶ COLLABORATION STRATEGY
Engage and motivate

One of the ways to inspire others is to take an interest in their development. People seem to become very motivated when they are working with a leader who is engaged with them in this way.

You can demonstrate your interest by arranging regular conversations with individual team members. These should be standalone discussions rather than just a casual, one-off question at the end of a meeting. Your attention will not only encourage the staff member, but will also ripple out through the team, as a motivated person always inspires others.

So often we get caught up in results, to the exclusion of the person who is delivering those results. That's not to say that results aren't important; the aim is to strike a balance between outcomes and team welfare. Showing interest in individual team members is always likely to deliver better results.

COACHING PRACTICE
Taking an interest

If you don't have regular one-on-one meetings with your team members, consider introducing this practice. Make notes at each meeting so that you can return to them at the next meeting.

Having a structured approach is very powerful. Scheduling regular catch-ups in your diary shows a commitment to each team member. For leaders there may be no more important practice.

QUESTIONS AND OBSERVATIONS

- What development opportunities do you see for each team member?
- Can you see areas where they can improve their collaboration skills? Is there an opportunity to encourage them to consider other perspectives and thereby influence their development on the cognitive line?
- Are they taking responsibility for their commitments?

Summary

We all have the potential to change ourselves and those around us by considering and modifying the ways we interact with other people. Adopting a more collaborative approach in our lives will bring all kinds of benefits, both psychological and practical.

In the workplace these will include an improved team culture, with a focus on delivering results. Developing a shared understanding of how team members work together will save time you might otherwise spend resolving misunderstandings, as team members will become much more adept at doing that themselves.

I am confident that the information in this book will support you in your development, and I invite you to share these practices and ideas with others. Making time to reflect on your leadership and try out new strategies will empower you to take responsibility for your own growth.

My wish for you is that ultimately you will be able to say, proudly and confidently: "I collaborate."

Good luck!

Acknowledgments

References to the book *The Collaborative Way®* and related concepts included with the kind permission of Lloyd Fickett.

To Sean Esjborn Hargens, thank you for your teaching and coaching.
To Lloyd Fickett, thank you for your teaching, mentoring and understanding.
To Doshin Nelson Roshi, thank you for your teaching and support and for introducing me to Lloyd.
To Joanne Hunt and Laura Divine, thank you for creating such a powerful coaching method at Integral Coaching Canada. I have built a successful business by applying your teaching.
To Paul Bennett for his sometimes challenging and always supportive leadership style. I learned a lot from you, Paul.
To David McAloney for being a visionary leader and investing in the development of your team in the midst of a crisis.
To Scott Forbes and Cathy Campbell, thank you so much for your support in preparing this book. I really appreciated your words of wisdom and expertise.

www.ingramcontent.com/pod-product-compliance
Lightning Source LLC
Chambersburg PA
CBHW061612220326
41598CB00024BC/3563